# the THING ABOUT MUMS

This edition copyright © 2001 Lion Publishing
Illustrations copyright © 2001 Kate Sheppard

Published by
**Lion Publishing plc**
Sandy Lane West, Oxford, England
www.lion-publishing.co.uk
ISBN 0 7459 4768 9

First edition 2001
10 9 8 7 6 5 4 3 2 1 0

**Acknowledgments**

34: I Corinthians 13:4, 7, taken from the *Holy Bible, New International Version*,
copyright © 1973, 1978, 1984 by International Bible Society. Used by permission.

Every effort has been made to trace and acknowledge copyright holders
of all the quotations in this book. We apologize for any errors or omissions
that may remain, and would ask those concerned to contact the publishers,
who will ensure that full acknowledgment is made in the future.

A catalogue record for this book is available
from the British Library

Typeset in Antique Olive Roman
Printed and bound in Malta

# The THING ABOUT MUMS

Compiled by Olivia Warburton

Illustrated by Kate Sheppard

LION
Giftlines

To a one-of-a-kind **mum**!

----------------------------------------

----------------------------------------

# What mums want

To live is so startling it leaves time for little else.

Emily Dickinson

More time

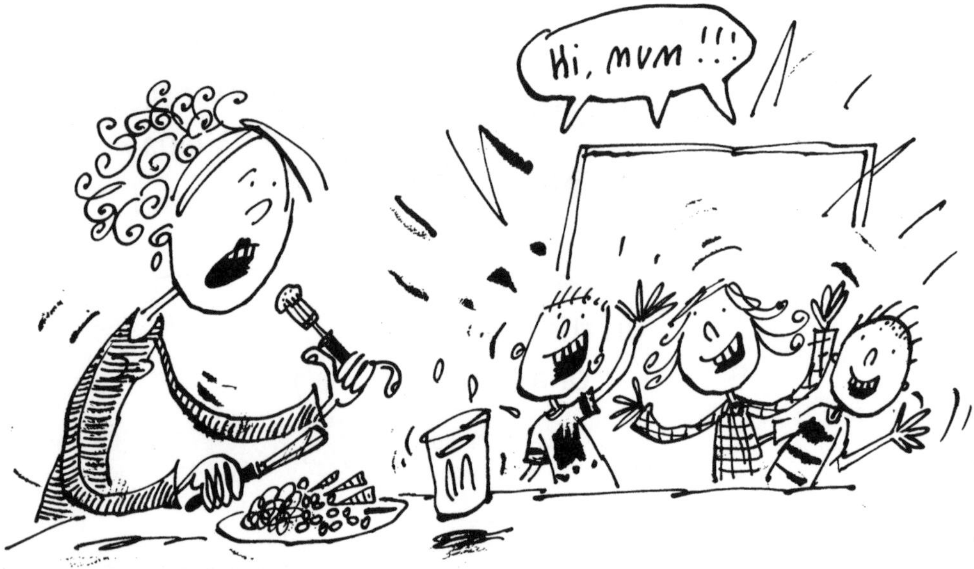
Hi, mum !!!

Time is an illusion.
Lunchtime doubly so.

Douglas Adams

Time flies like an
arrow; fruit flies
like a banana.

Groucho Marx

I'll
be with you
in the squeezing
of a lemon.

Oliver Goldsmith

● ● ● ● ● ● ● ● ● ● ● ● ● ● ● ● ● ● ● ●

I wondered how my children saw me. Did they see this confused person, trying to juggle home, work, kids, husband, dogs, cats etc... or did they see something else?

Lynn Massey-Davis

Three stages in a parent's life: nutrition, dentition, tuition.

Marcelene Cox

● ● ● ● ● ● ● ● ● ● ● ● ● ●

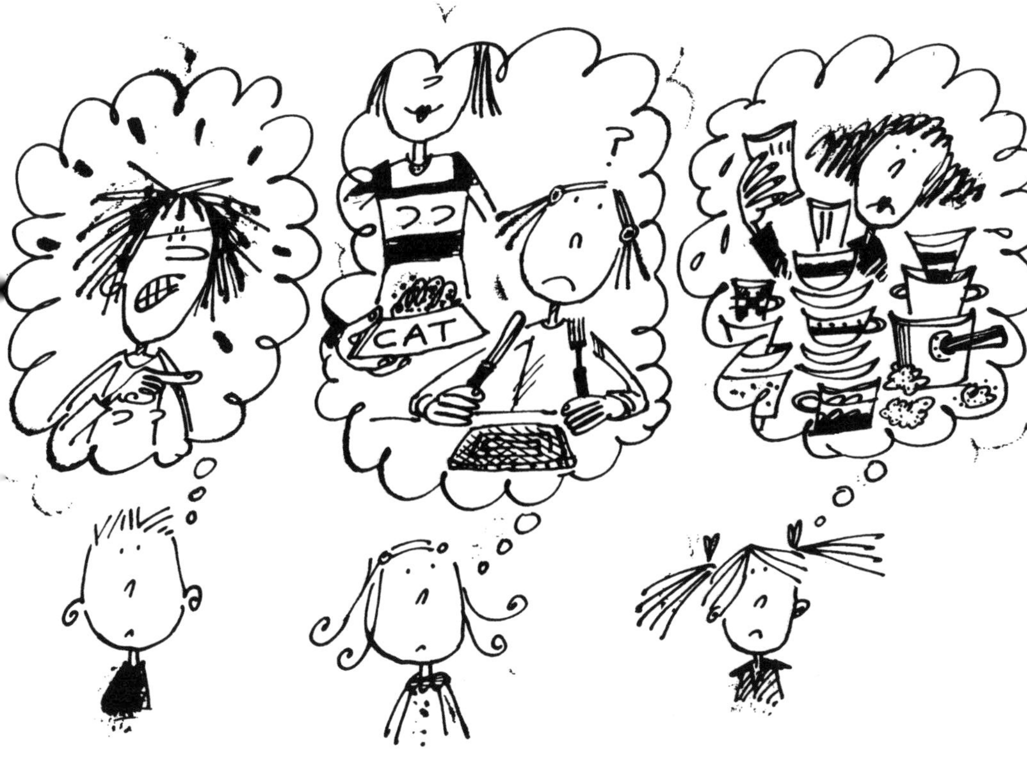
CAT

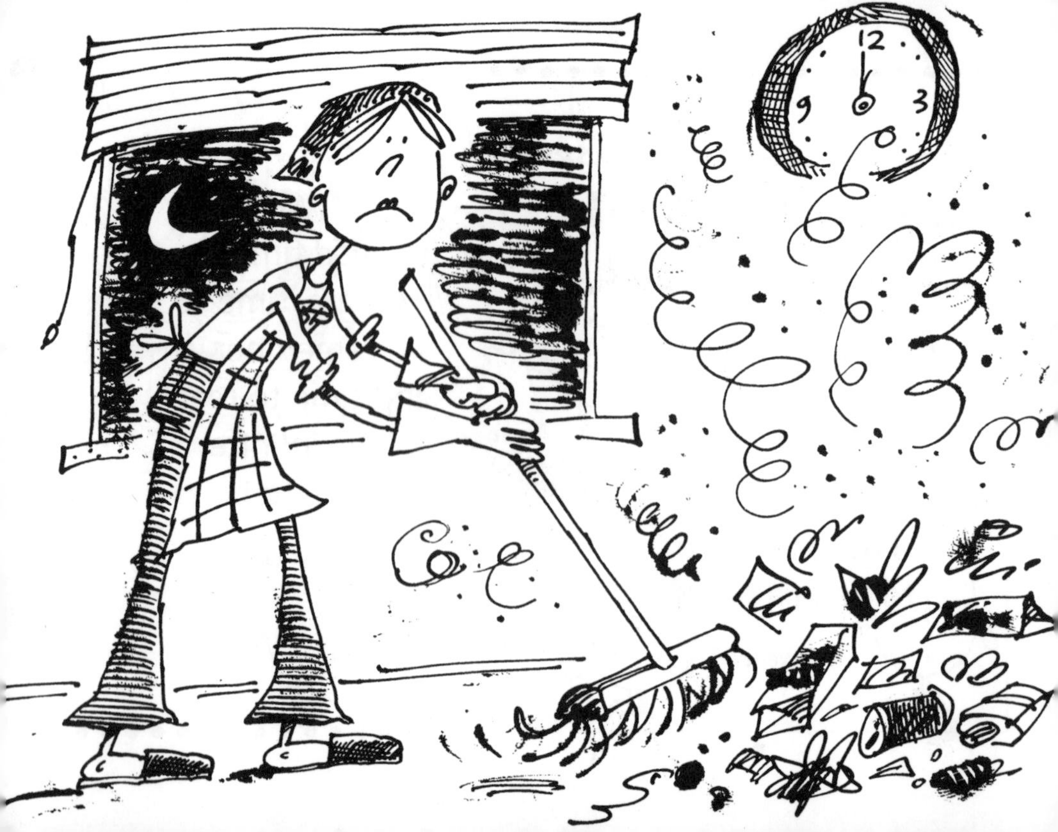

• • • • • • • • • • • • • • • • • • • •

Conran's Law of Housework
— it expands to fill the
time available plus half
an hour.

Shirley Conran

I have no time
to be in a hurry.

John Wesley

We
need time to
dream, time to
remember,
and time to reach
the infinite.
Time to be.

Gladys Taber

• • • • • • • • • • • • • • • •

The amount of sleep required by the average person is about five minutes more.

Wilson Misner

Sometimes the best way to deal with everyday life is to lie down and take a nap.

Joyce Bartels

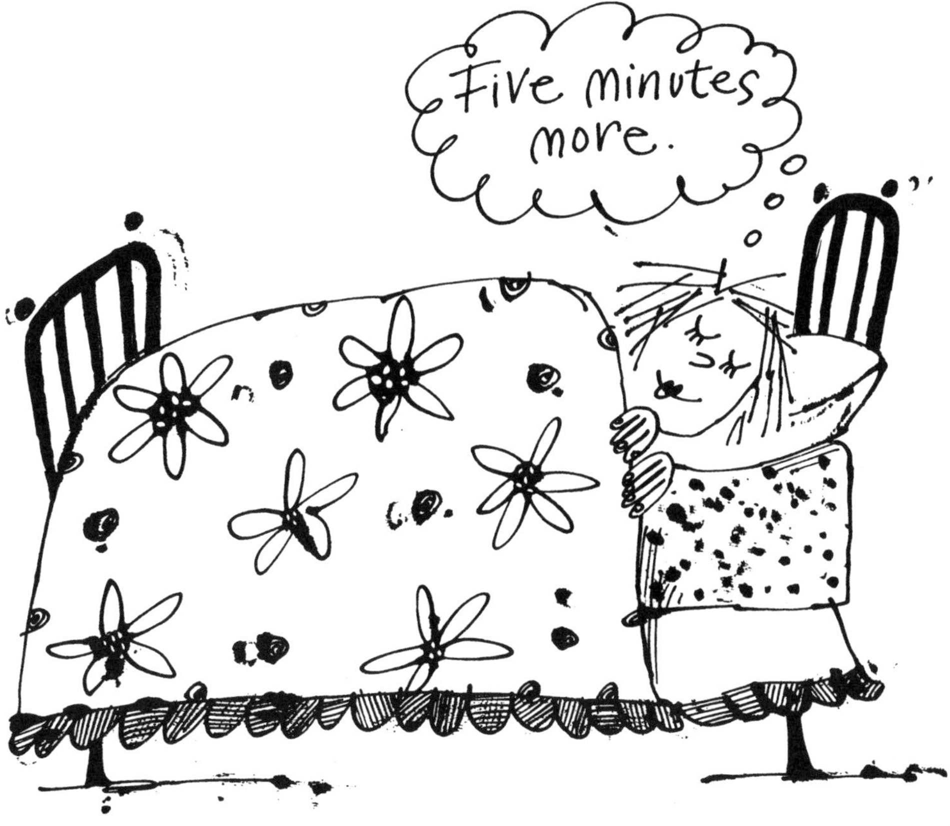
Five minutes more.

Maternal love: a miraculous substance which God multiplies as he divides it.

Victor Hugo

More space

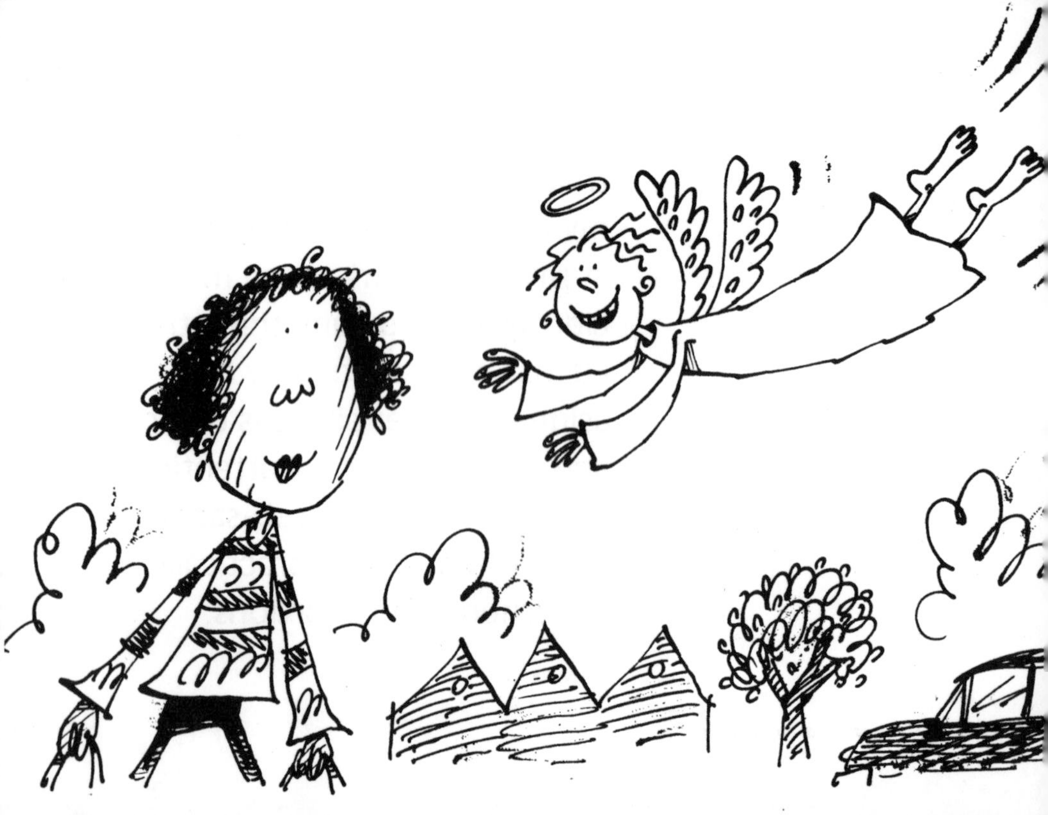

There was a pause — just long enough for an angel to pass, flying slowly.

Ronald Firbank

It took me years to realize that every time I interrupted my mother to ask her to look at my homework, wash my clothes or find something that I'd lost, and she quietly laid aside whatever she was doing and gave me her full attention, she was displaying self-sacrifice and self-control of practically superhuman proportions.

Emily, 25

The mother-child relationship is paradoxical. It requires the most intense love on the mother's side, yet this very love must help the child grow away from the mother to become independent.

Erich Fromm

Silence is the language of God.

Dag Hammerskjøld

You can learn many things from children. How much patience you have, for instance.

Franklin P. Jones

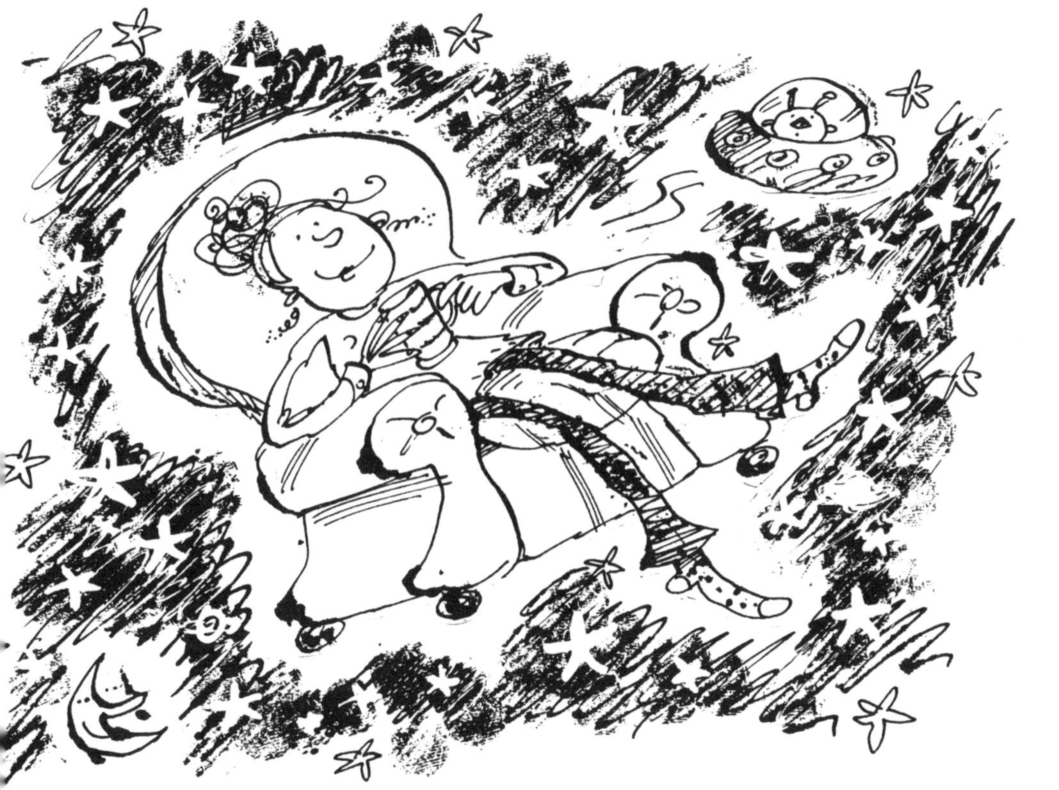

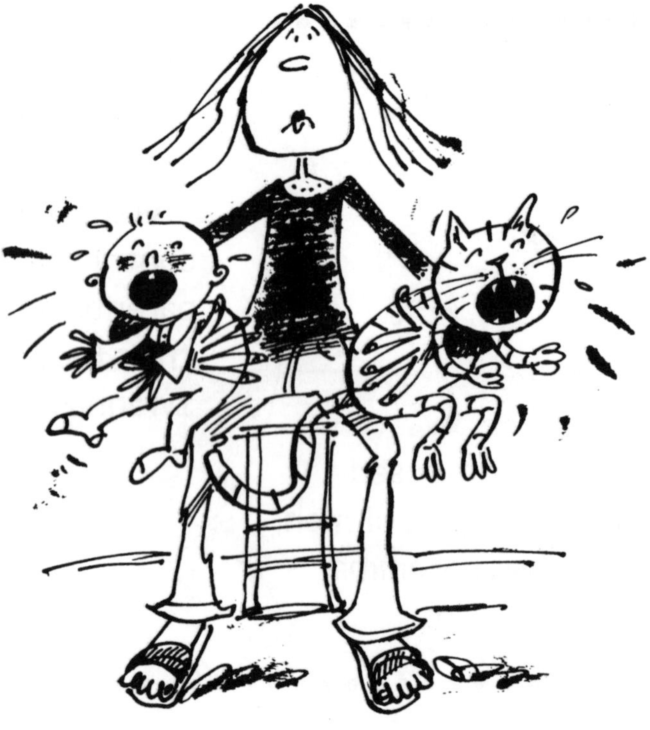

*Every baby needs a lap.*

Henry Robin

A family is a unit composed not only of children but of men, women, an occasional animal, and the common cold.

Ogden Nash

Children today are tyrants. They contradict their parents, gobble their food, and tyrannize their teachers.

Socrates

Don't tell me that worry doesn't do any good. I know better. The things I worry about don't happen.

Author unknown

A
ruffled mind makes
a restless pillow.

Charlotte Brontë

Everything's getting on top of me. I can't switch off. I've got a self-cleaning oven — I have to get up in the night to see if it's doing it.

Victoria Wood

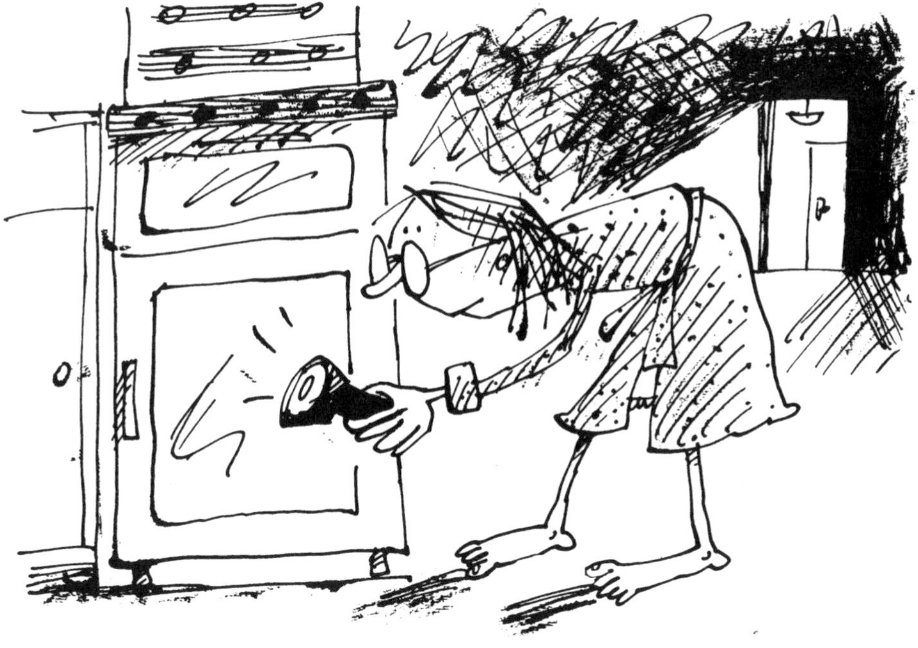

In the dim background of our mind we know what we ought to be doing, but somehow we cannot start.

William James

More energy

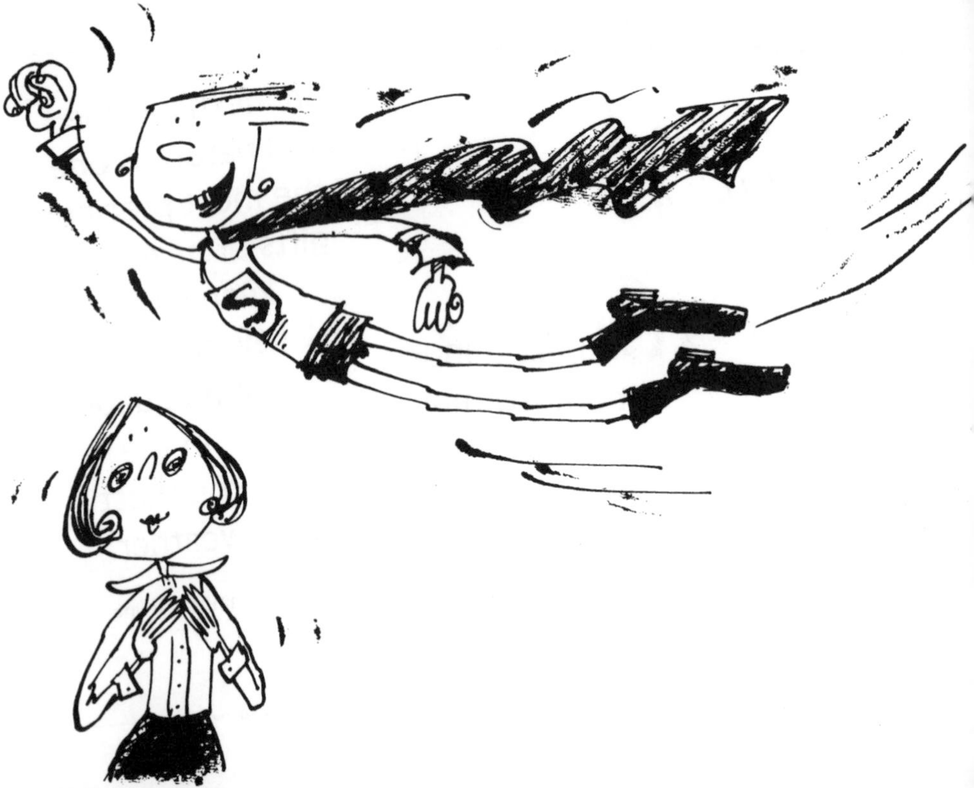

Mother love is a
powerful thing.
You wouldn't
believe
what you
can do
with her
willing
you on!

Patricia Smith

The best thing about my mother is her unwillingness to give up.

Sophie, 15

An inexhaustible good nature is one of the most precious gifts of heaven, keeping the mind smooth and equable in the roughest weather.

Washington Irving

My mother had a great deal of trouble with me, but I think she enjoyed it.

Mark Twain

I don't know why I did it, I don't know why I enjoyed it, and I don't know why I'll do it again.

Bart Simpson

There are only two things a child will share willingly: communicable diseases and his mother's age.

Author unknown

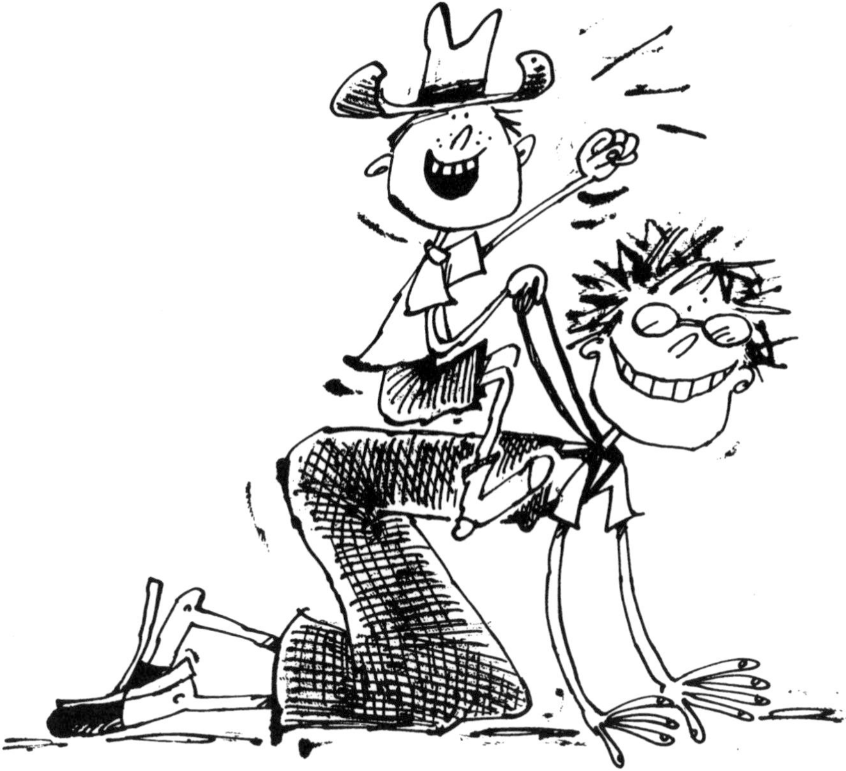

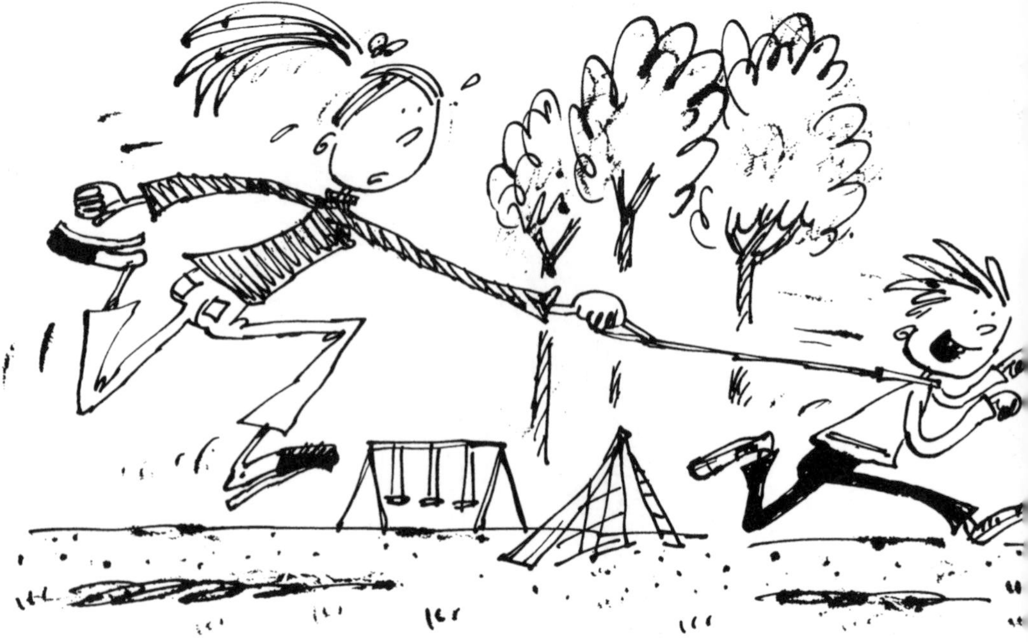

Small boys are like puppies: they need to be exercised on a regular basis.

Juliet Janvrin

A child develops individuality long before he discovers taste.

Erma Bombeck

Adolescence is a period of rapid changes. Between the ages of twelve and seventeen, for example, a parent ages as much as twenty years.

Author unknown

Love is patient, love is kind. It always protects, always trusts, always hopes, always perseveres.

The Bible

There was never a child so lovely but his mother was glad to get him asleep.

Ralph Waldo Emerson

I found my mother sitting on the coverlet, and leaning over me. I fell asleep in her arms after that, and slept soundly.

Charles Dickens

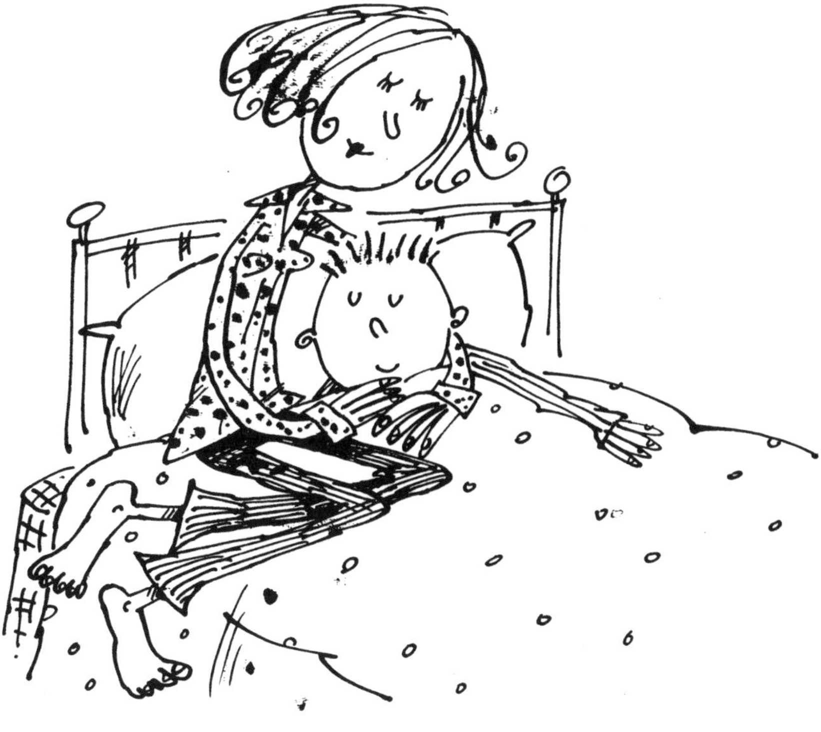

Imagination is more important than knowledge.

Albert Einstein

Some good ideas

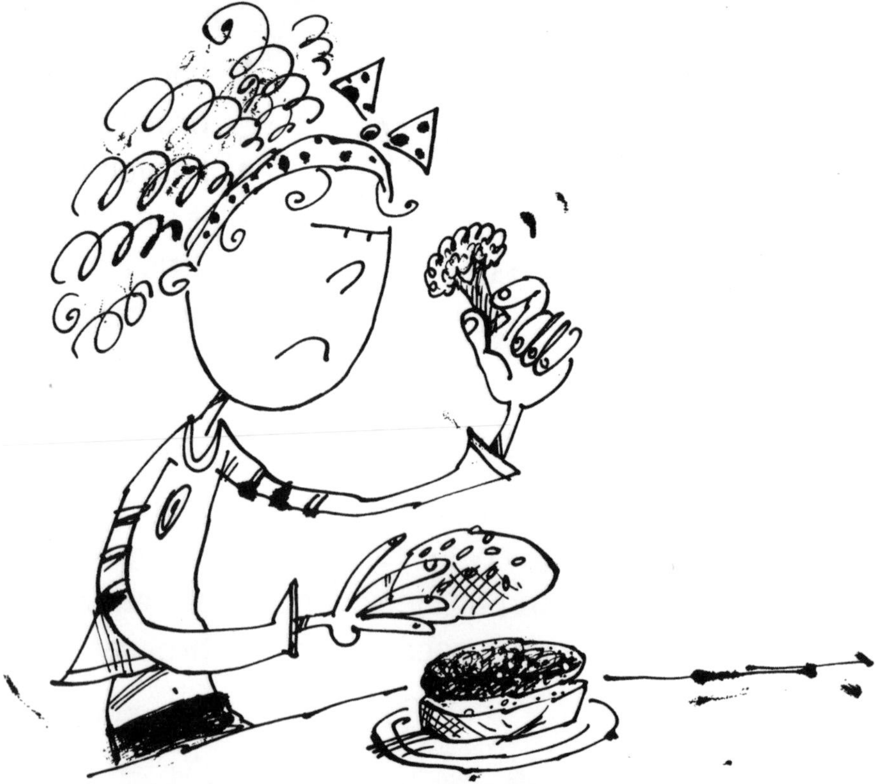

I hate it when my mum disguises broccoli and stuff in burgers and tricks me into eating vegetables.

Zoe, 7

I do not like broccoli. And I haven't liked it since I was a little kid and my mother made me eat it. And I'm President of the United States and I'm not going to eat any more broccoli.

George Bush

The most remarkable thing about my mother is that for thirty years she served the family nothing but leftovers. The original meal has never been found.

Calvin Trillin

A child of five would
understand this.
Send someone to
fetch a child of five.

Groucho Marx

You know children
are growing up
when they start
asking questions
that have answers.

John J. Plomp

The
only interesting answers are
those which destroy the question.

Susan Sontag

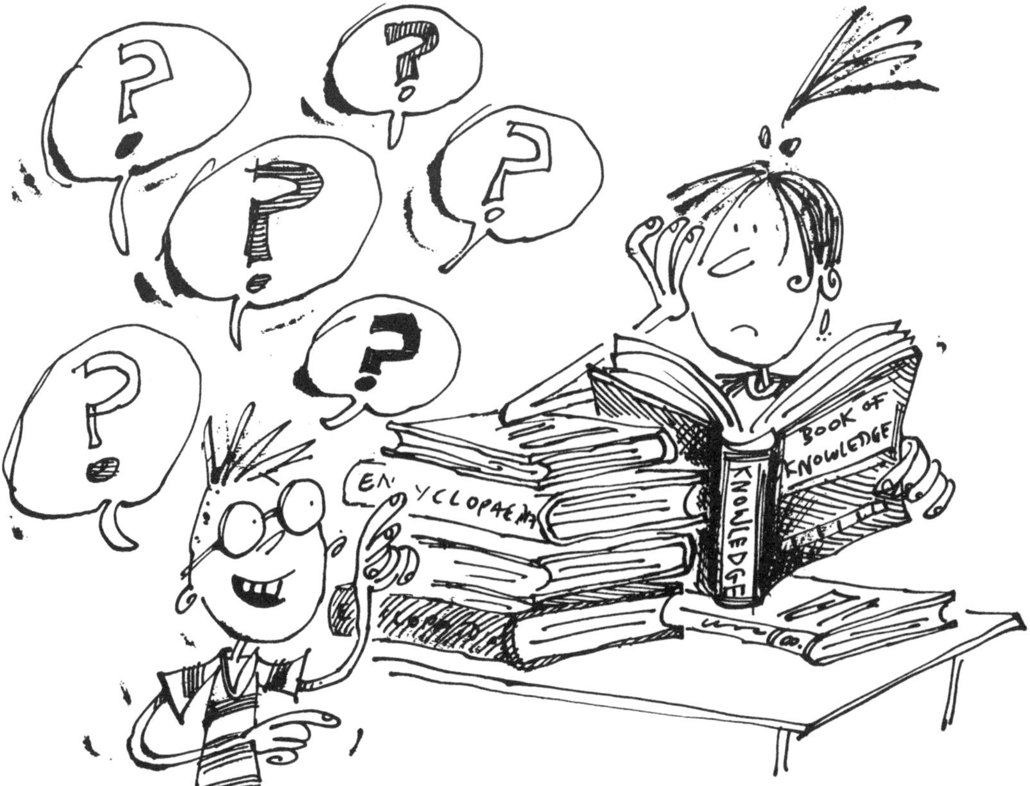
BOOK OF KNOWLEDGE
KNOWLEDGE

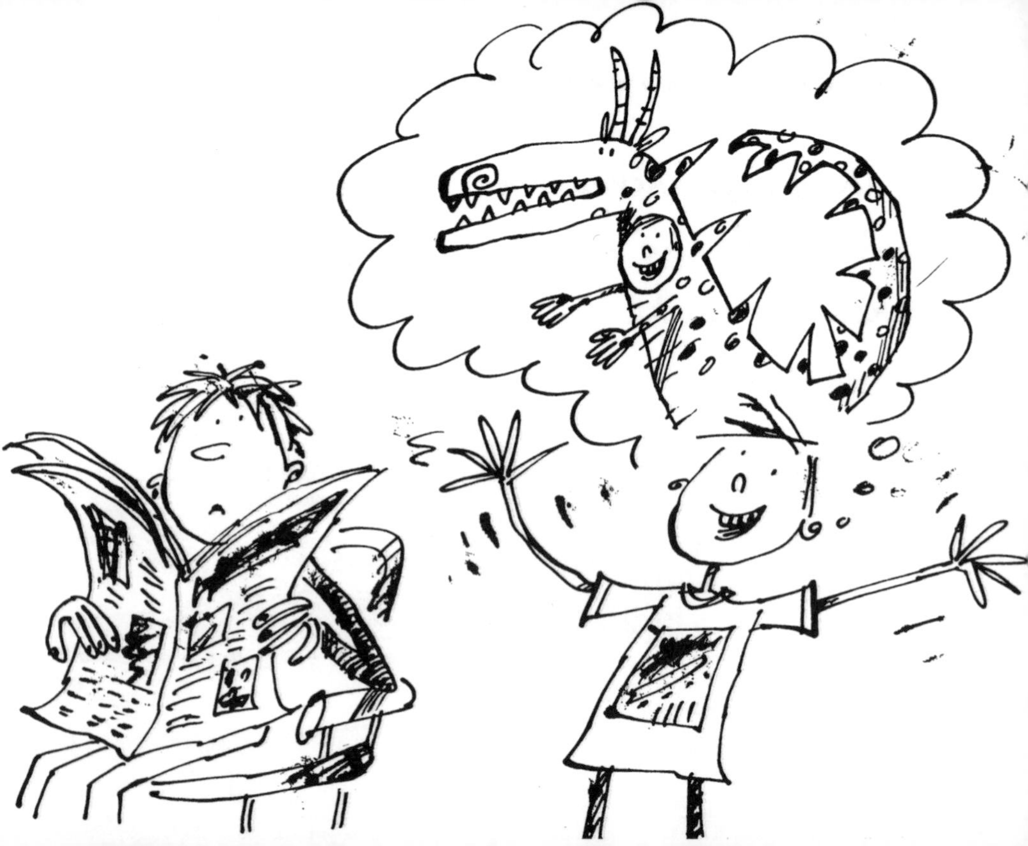

How the busy, uncreative parent dreads the words, 'We have to make a costume'!

Juliet Janvrin

Just when ideas fail, a word comes in to save the situation.

Johann Wolfgang von Goethe

Necessity is the mother of invention.

English proverb

Parents learn
a lot from
children
about
coping
with
life.

Muriel Spark

Anything which parents have not learned from experience they can now learn from their children.

Author unknown

My childhood should have taught me lessons for my own parenthood, but it didn't.

Bill Cosby

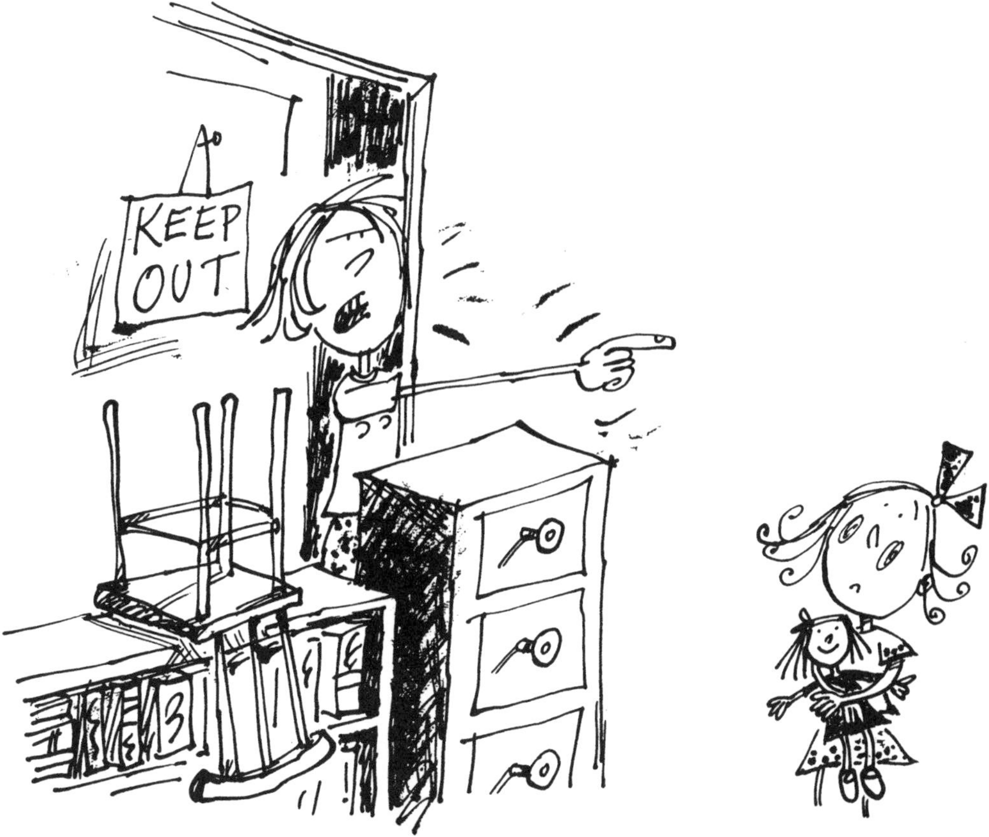
KEEP OUT

If you want to recapture your youth, just cut off his allowance.

Al Bernstein

Basic cooperation

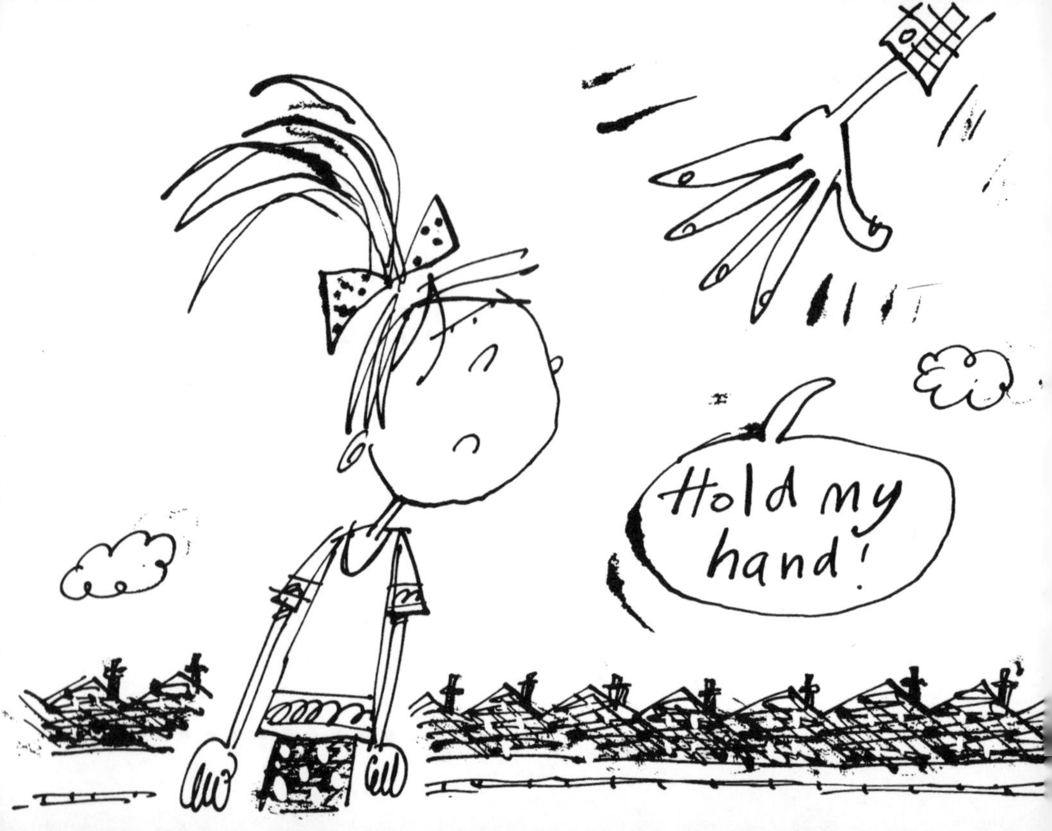
Hold my hand!

I never did, never did, never did like,
'Now take care, dear!'
I never did, never did, never did want,
'Hold my hand';
I never did, never did, never did think much of,
'Not up there, dear!'
It's no good saying it. They don't understand.

A.A. Milne

The secret of dealing successfully with a child is not to be its parent.

Mel Lazarus

Setting an example for your children takes all the fun out of middle age.

William Feather

She looked mild, but appearances were deceptive. Sometimes it was time to be elsewhere.

Billy Dunn

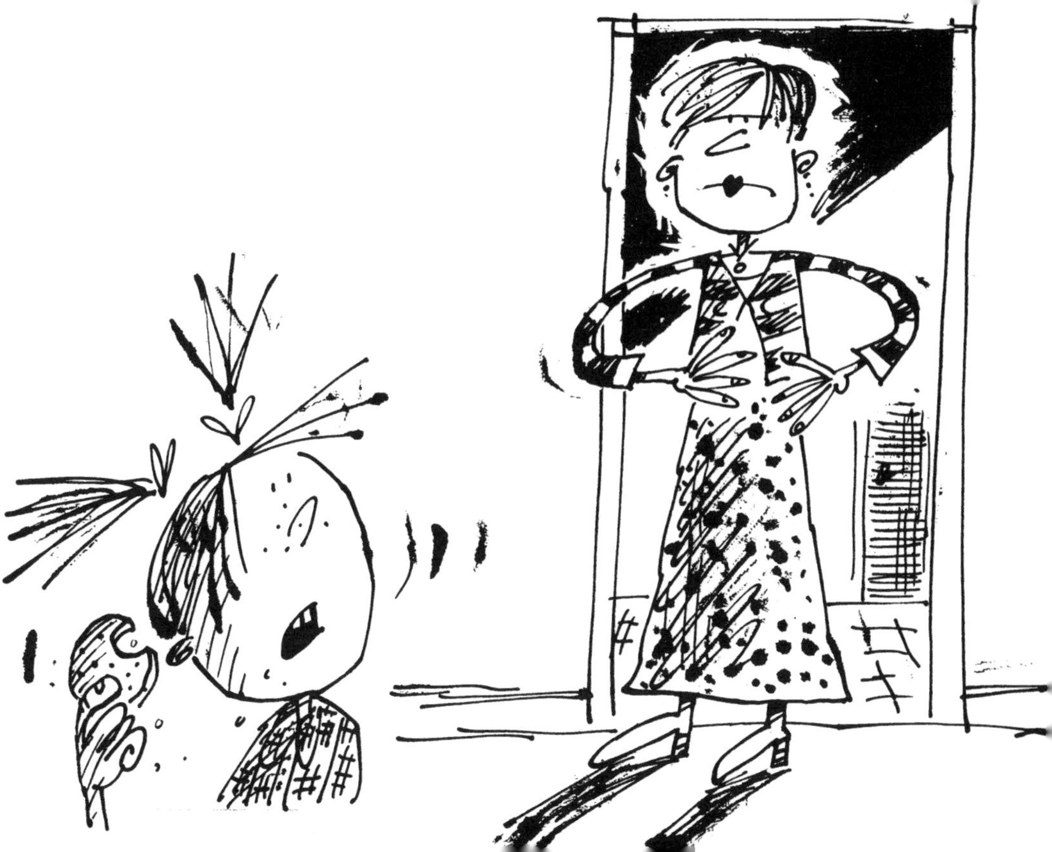

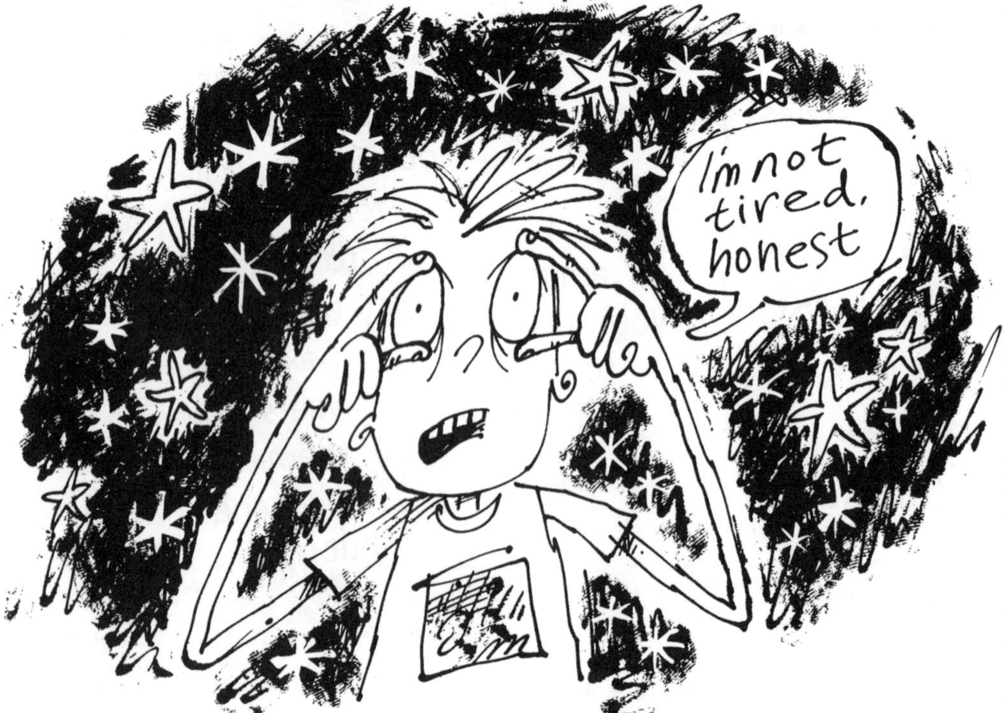
I'm not tired, honest

The hardest people
to convince
they are at
retirement
age are
children
at bedtime.

Shannon Fife

I
am not
young enough
to know
everything.

Oscar Wilde

We spend the first
twelve months of
our children's lives
teaching them
to walk and
talk and the
next twelve
years telling
them to sit
down and
shut up.

Phyllis Diller

The best thing about my mum is the way she understands me and makes me feel more like a friend than a daughter. Even when something goes wrong, we can still laugh about it.

Jenni, 14

Parenting is not logical. Life is filled with disagreement, opposition, illusion, irrational thinking, miracle, meaning, surprise, and wonder.

Jeanne Elium and Don Elium

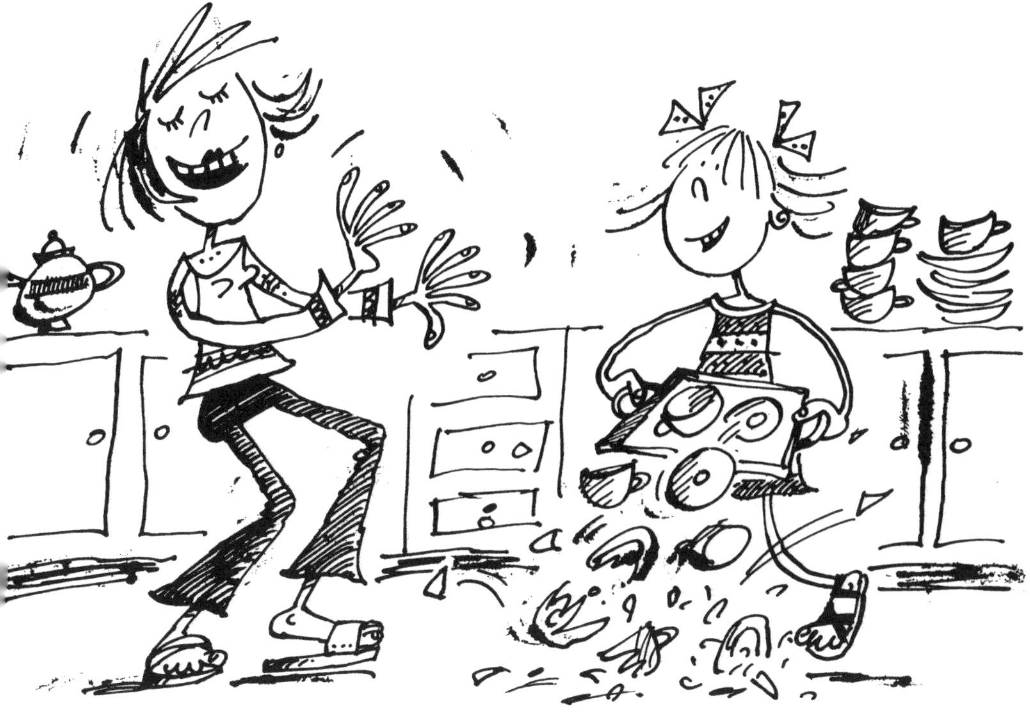

This above all:
to thine own self
be true.

William Shakespeare

Freedom to be

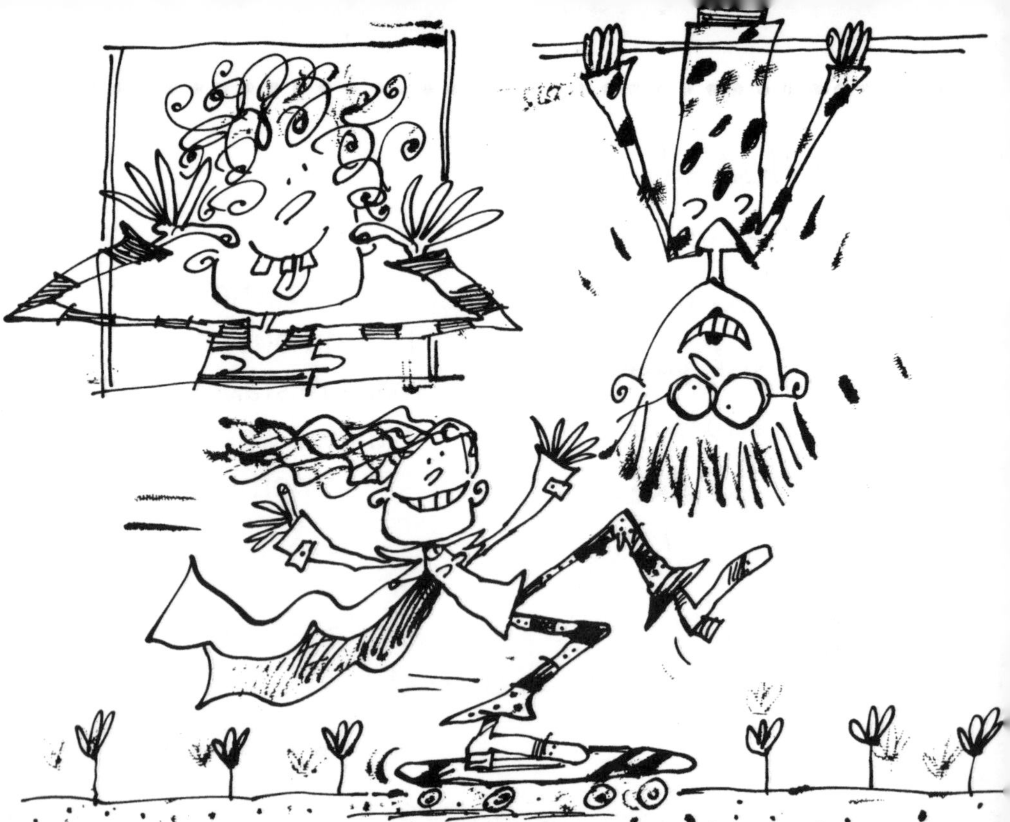

I believe that always, or almost always, in all childhoods and in all the lives that follow them, the mother represents madness. Our mothers always remain the strangest, craziest people we've ever met.

Marguerite Duras

It was when I found out I could make mistakes that I knew I was on to something.

Ornette Coleman

I've always wanted to ask you, mum, why did you make me wear so many clothes when it was cold?

Mike Yaconelli

It is a fact of life that mums react badly to odd socks and dirty mugs. Much pain and stress can be easily avoided by grasping this early on.

James, 30

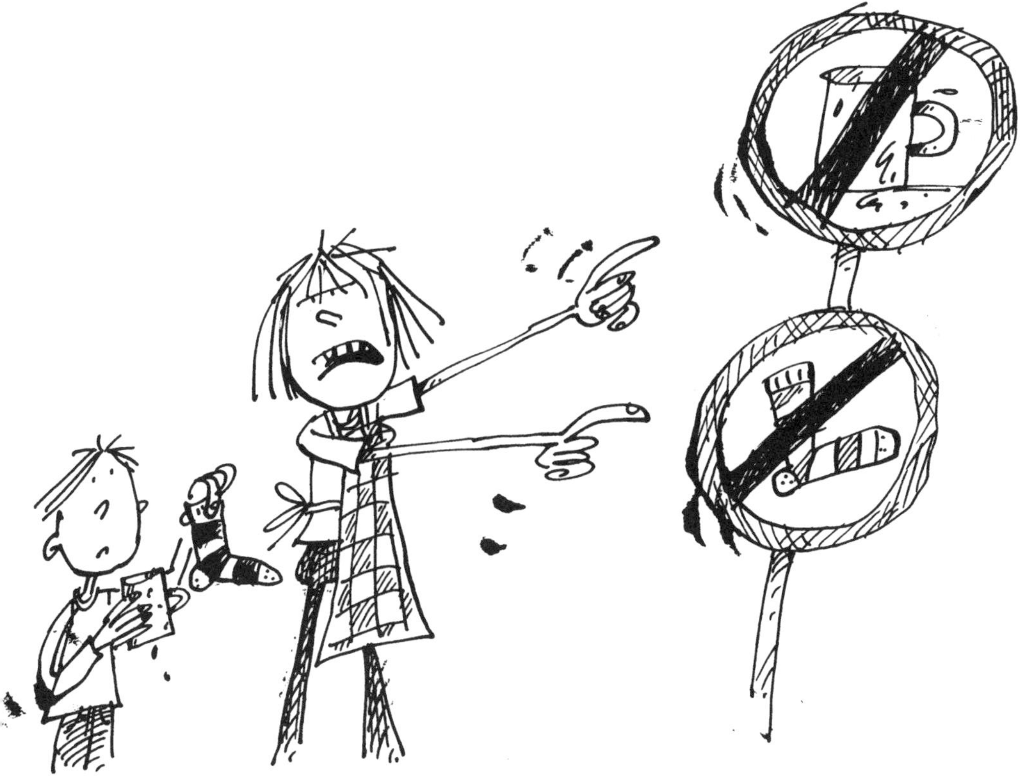

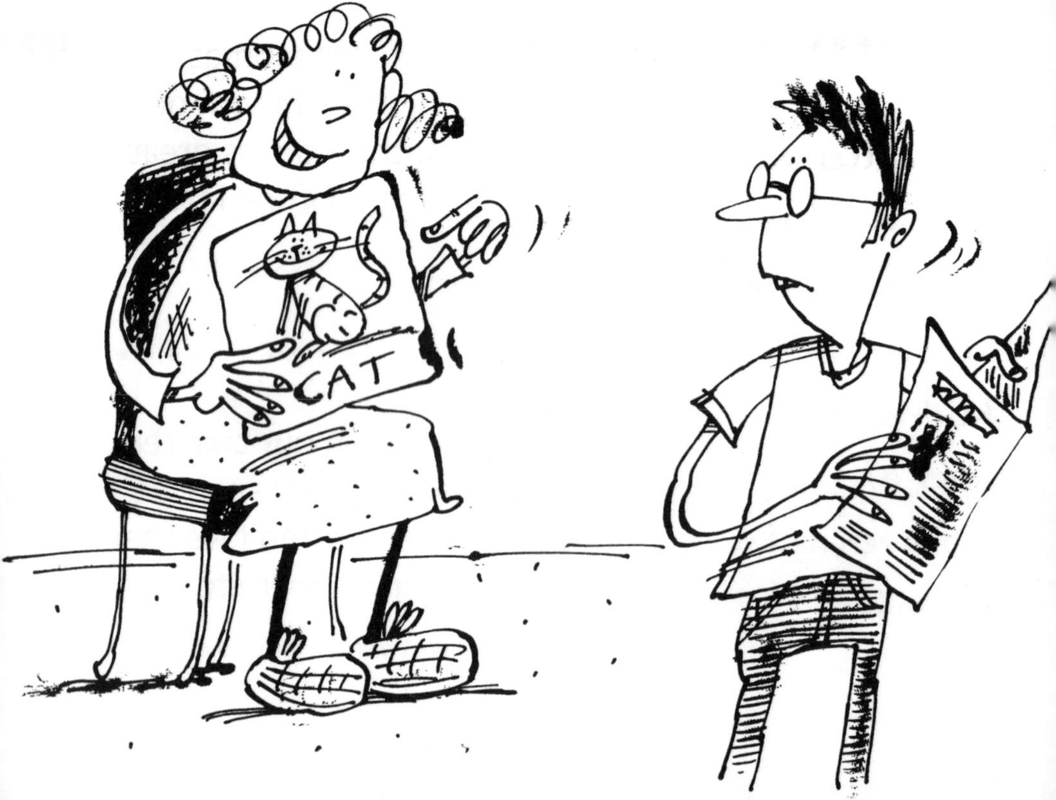
CAT

• • • • • • • • • • • • • • • • • •

No matter how old a mother is, she watches her middle-aged children for signs of improvement.

Florida Scott-Maxwell

Sometimes the strength of motherhood is greater than natural forces.

Barbara Kingsolver

• • • • • • • • • • • • • • • • • • • •

We can't form our children on our own concepts; we must take them and love them as God gives them to us.

Johann Wolfgang von Goethe

Birthdays are very important to mums. From the ends of the earth they will phone to tell you that Great-Uncle George's birthday is tomorrow and remind you to send a card.

Kirsty, 23

The mother of Columbus: 'I don't care what you've discovered, Christopher. You still could have written!'

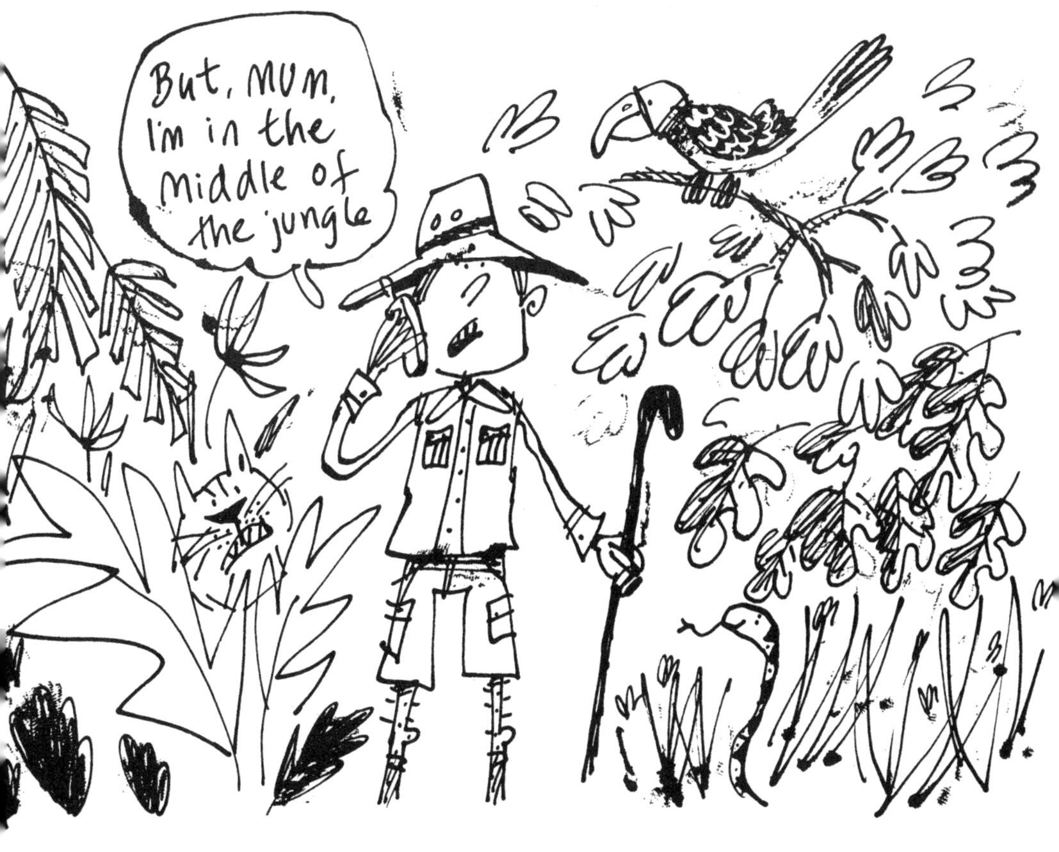
But, MUM, I'm in the middle of the jungle

No problem is so big
and complicated that it
can't be run away from.

Charles Schultz

# Coping strategies

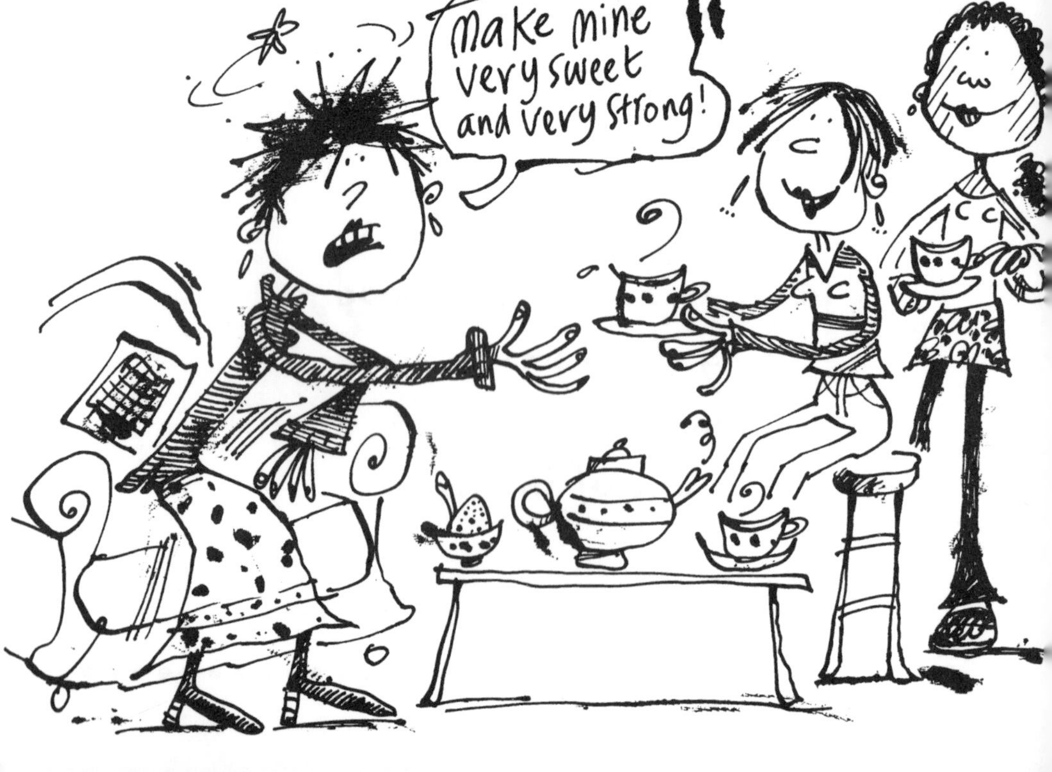
Make mine very sweet and very strong!

The intelligent mum takes care to have a few good coping strategies in place. Tea with friends is one of them.

She develops other interests.

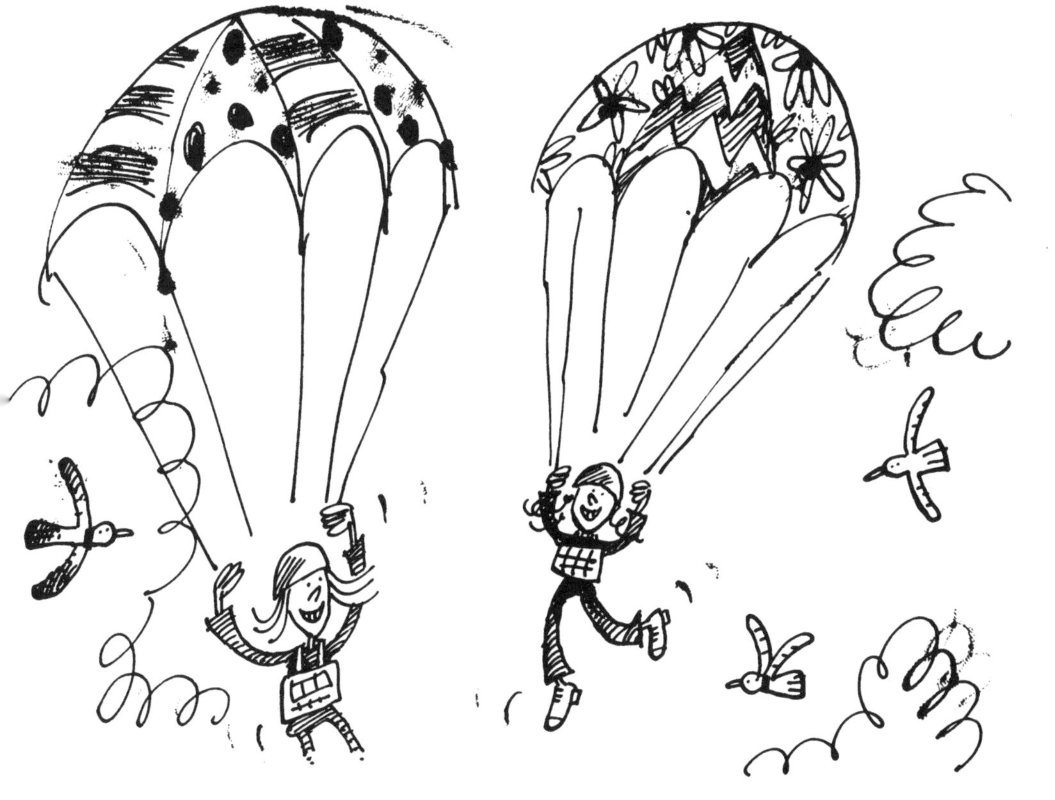

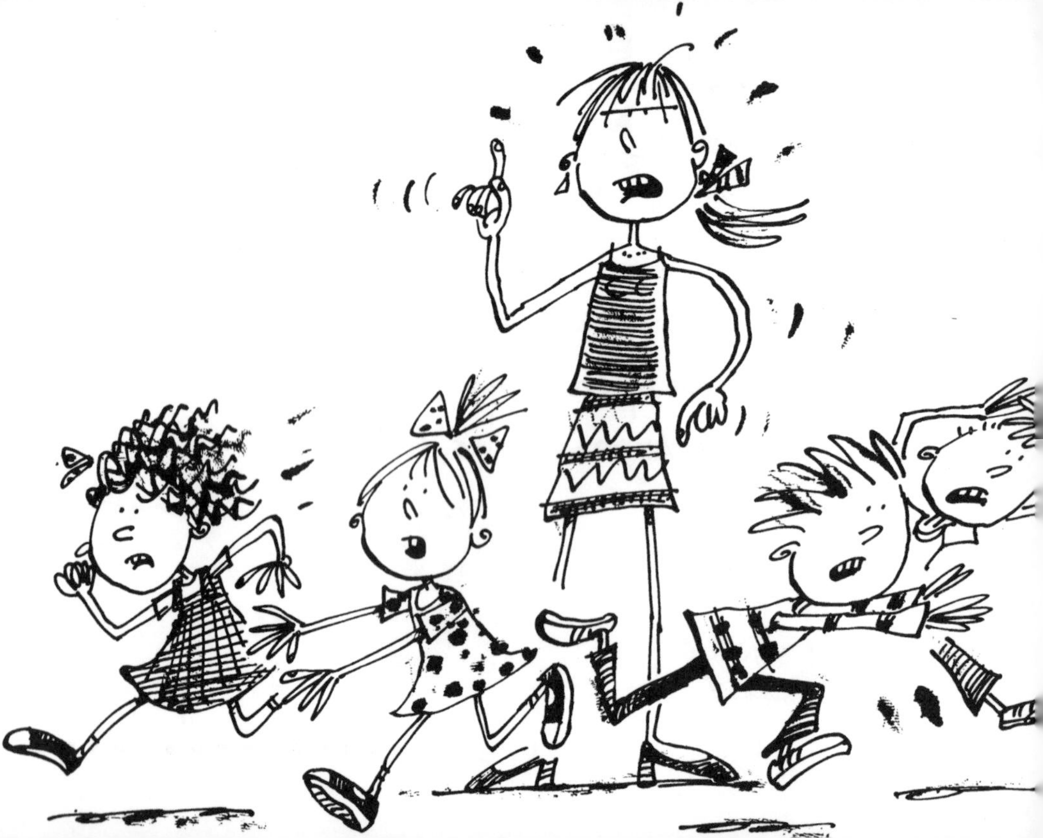

Occasionally
she speaks her mind,
and everyone runs for cover.

And when all else fails, she curls up with a good book.

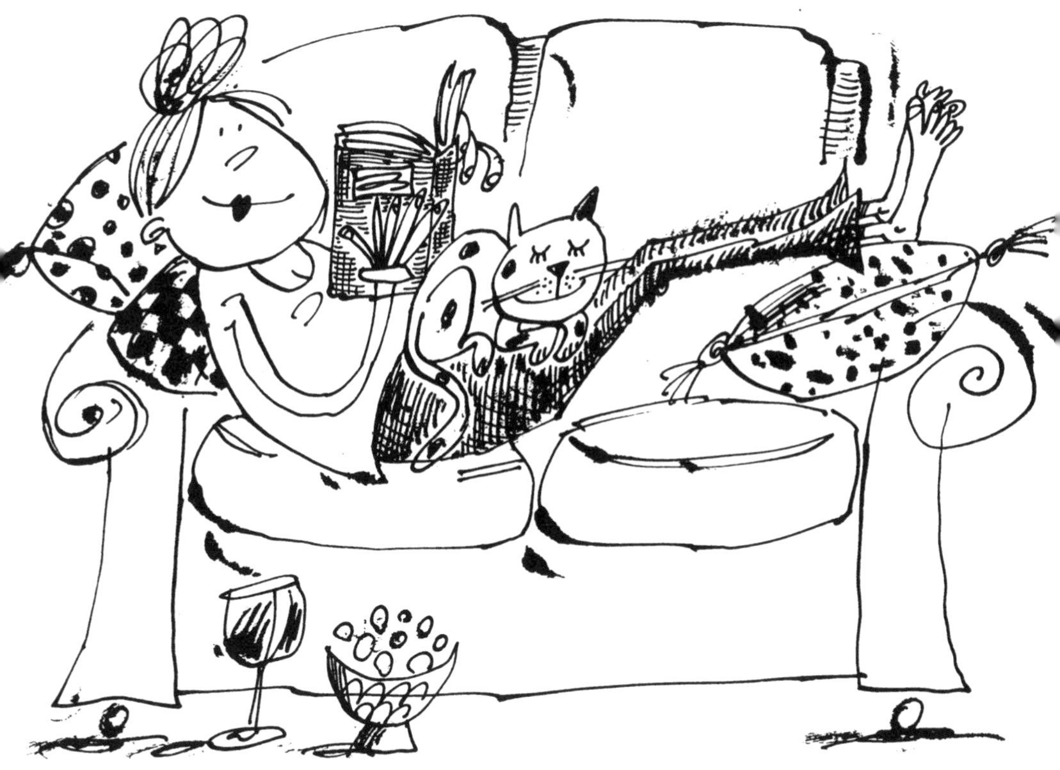

The family
is one of nature's
masterpieces.

George Santayana

Domestic harmony

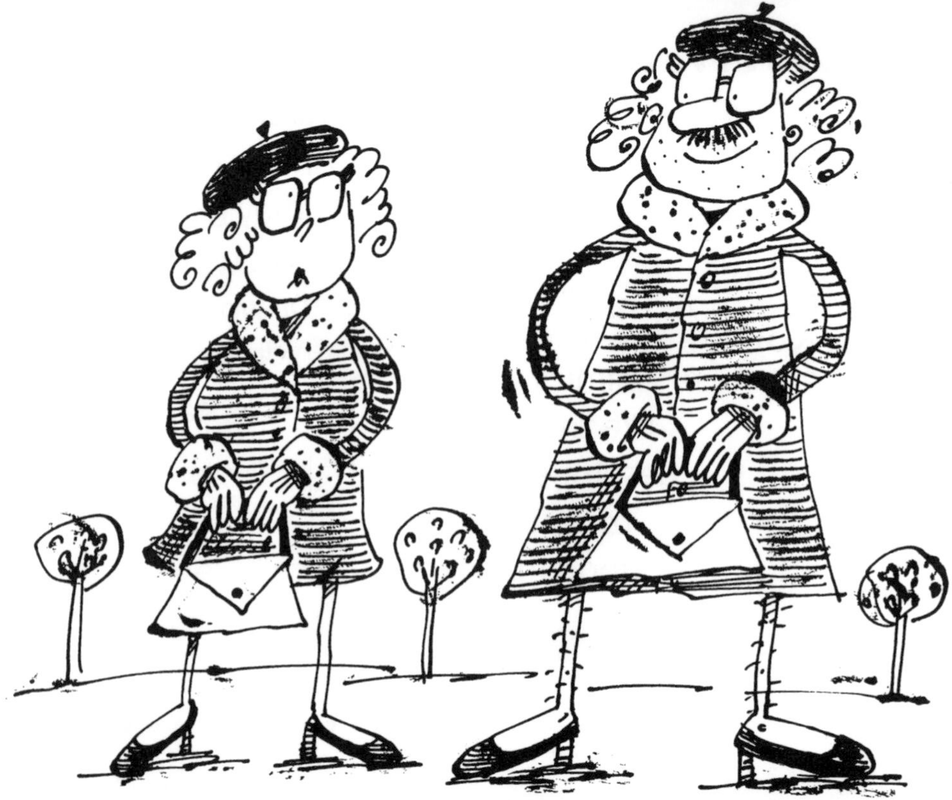

Don't try to make children grow up to be like you or they may do it.

Russell Baker

Children are natural mimics who act like their parents despite every effort to teach them good manners.

Author unknown

Children seldom misquote you. In fact, they usually repeat word for word what you shouldn't have said.

Author unknown

Home is not the one tame place in a world of adventure; it is the one wild place in a world of rules and set tasks.

G.K. Chesterton

Home interprets heaven. Home is heaven for beginners.

Charles H. Parkhurst

There will be times in life when impossibility is felt, but then there are dreams — and dreams allow us possibility.

Jeffrey David Lang

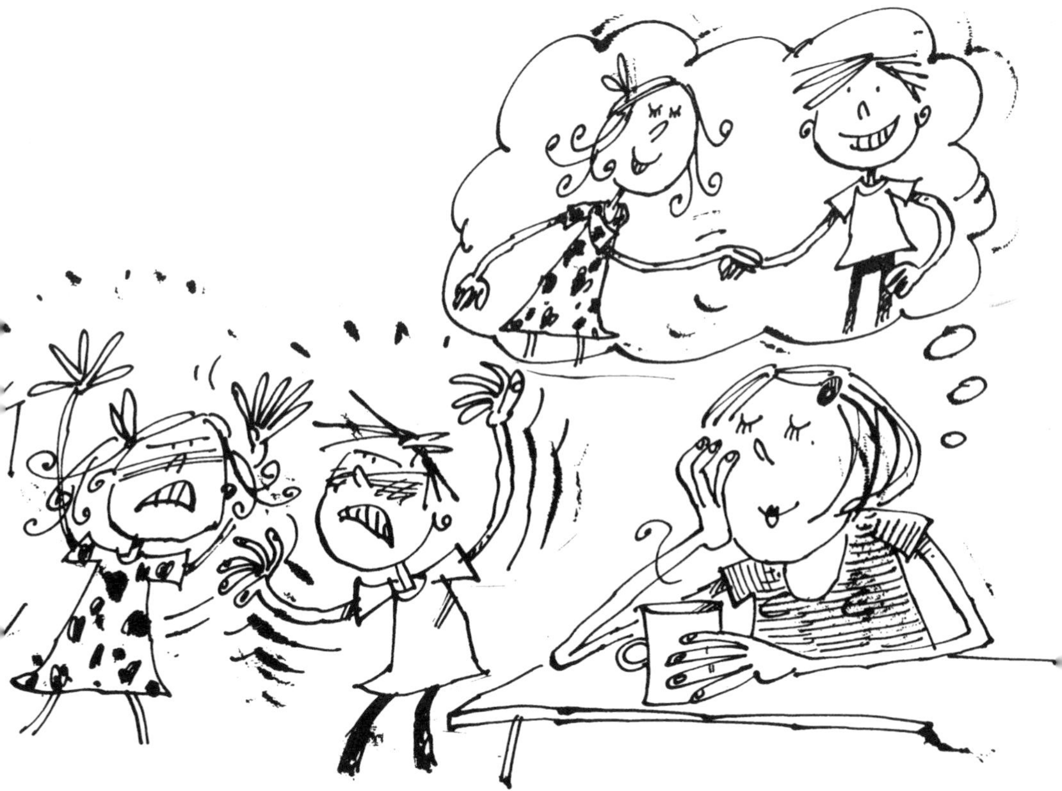

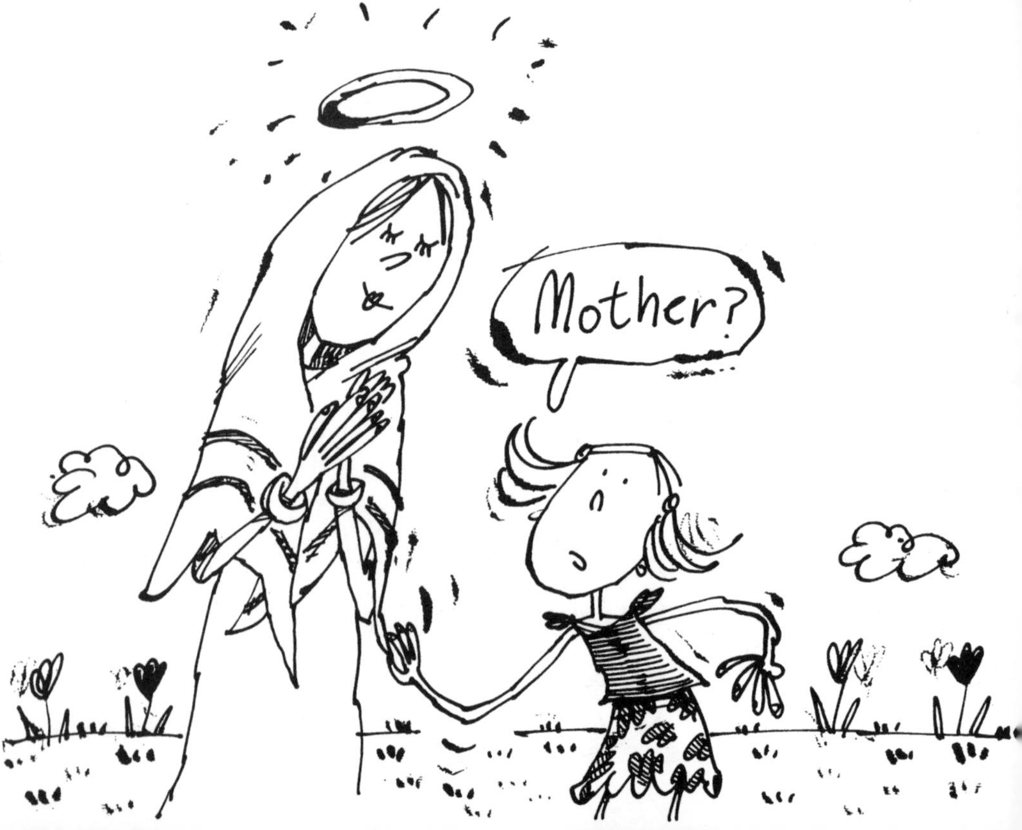
Mother?

Love begins by taking care of the closest ones – the ones at home.

Mother Teresa
of Calcutta

My mum always wants to be like Mother Teresa.

Deborah, 11

My mother used to say, 'He who angers you, conquers you!' But my mother was a saint.

Elizabeth Kenny

There is a mother's heart
in the heart of God.

Celtic saying

• • • • • • • • • • • • • • • • • • • • •

Never lend your car
to anyone to whom
you have given birth.

Erma Bombeck

Who is it that
loves me and will
love me for ever
with an affection
which no chance,
no misery, no
crime of mine can
do away? — It is
you, my mother.

Thomas Carlyle

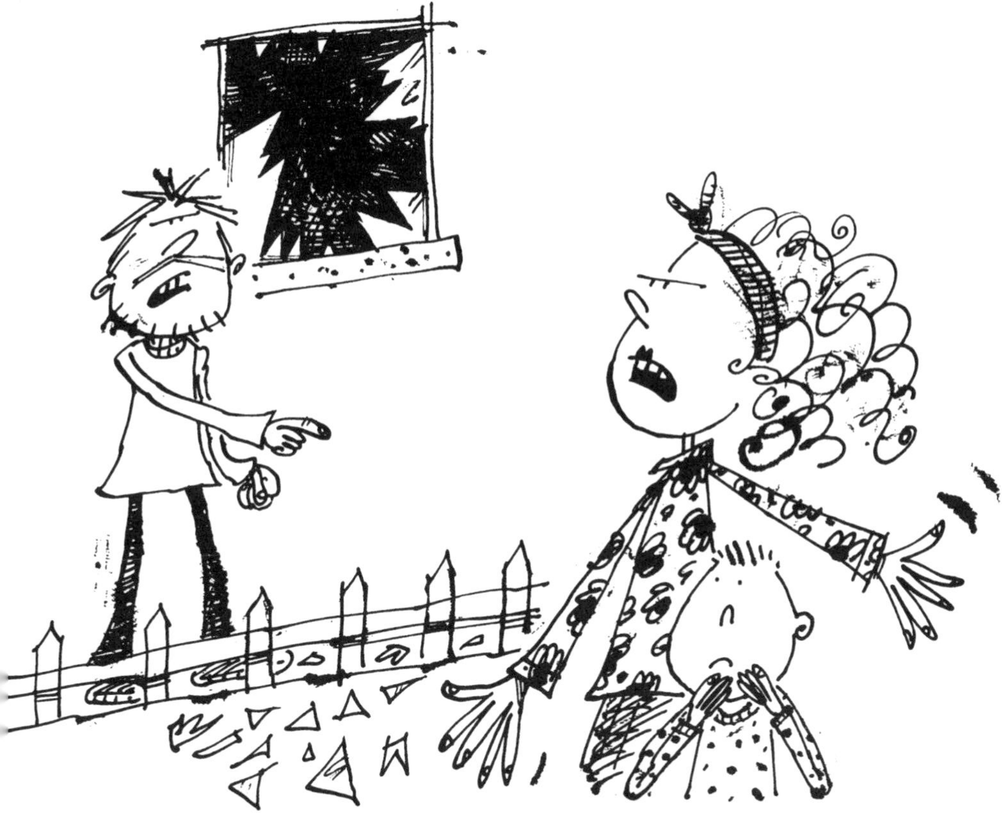

The soul
is healed by being
with children.

Fyodor Dostoevsky

Lots of love

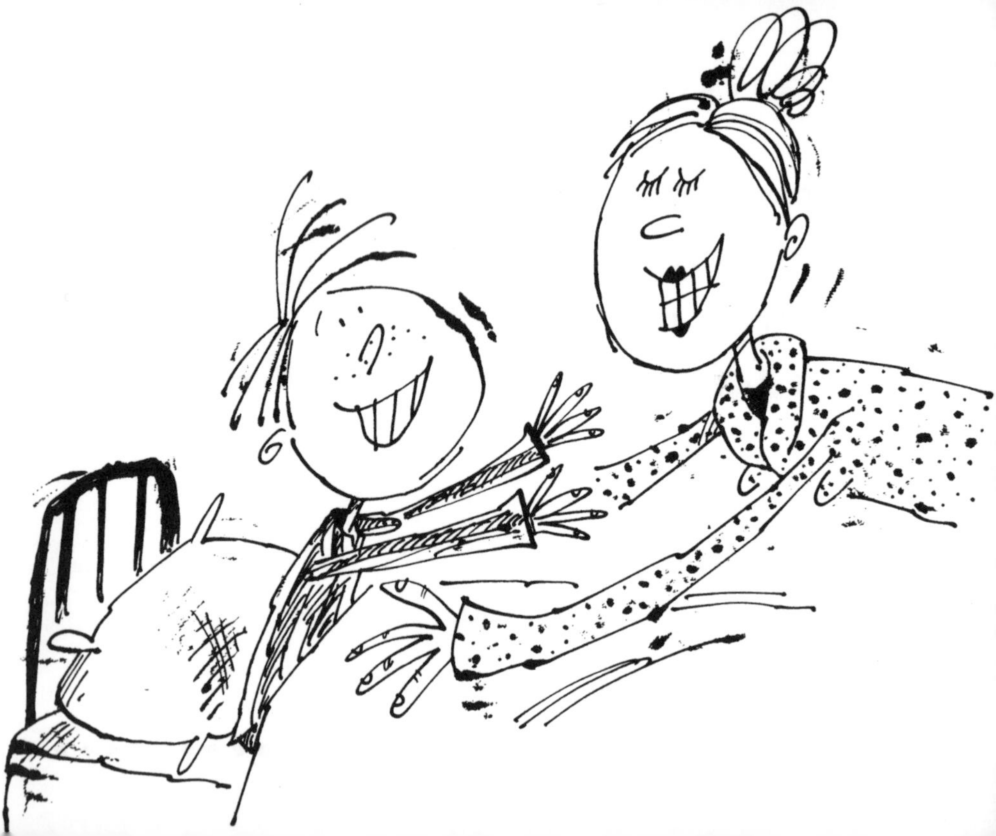

I think my life began with waking up and loving my mother's face.

George Eliot

The potential possibilities of any child are the most intriguing and stimulating in all creation.

Ray L. Wilbur

Children reinvent your world for you.

Susan Sarandon

Mothers are great
at keeping in touch
— even if they do
always seem to
phone at mealtimes.

Emma, 19

A
slight touch
of amusement
towards those we
love keeps our
affections for them
from turning flat.

Logan P. Smith

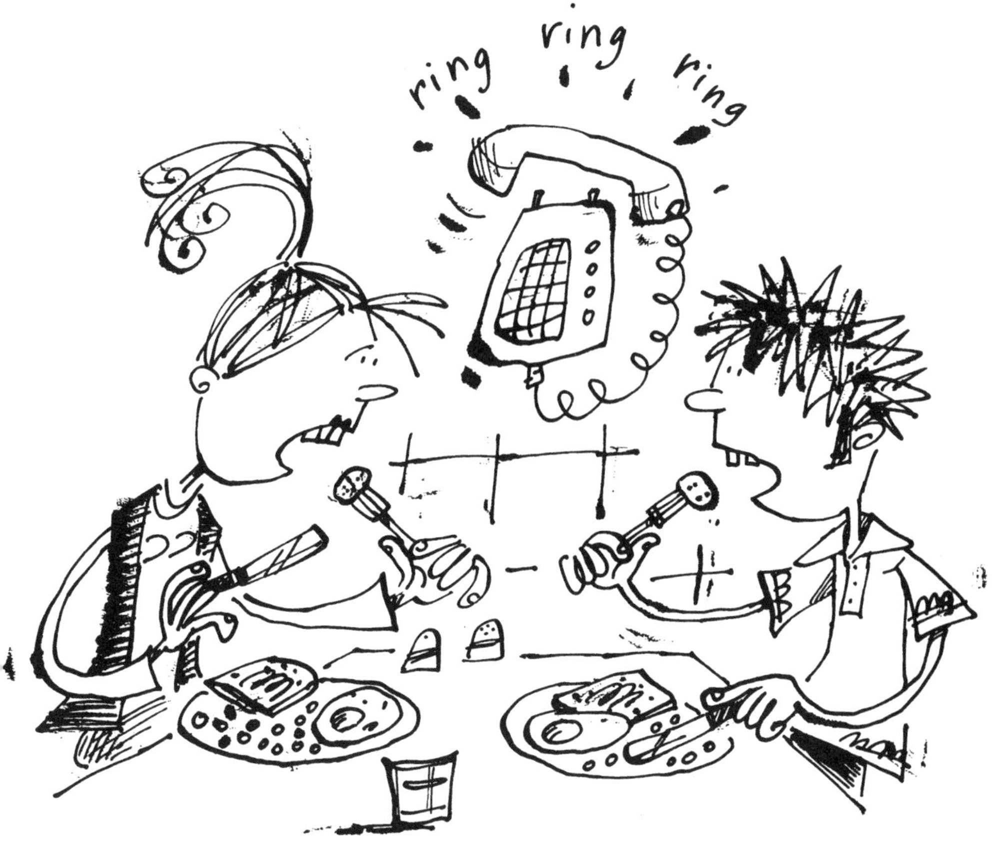
ring ring ring

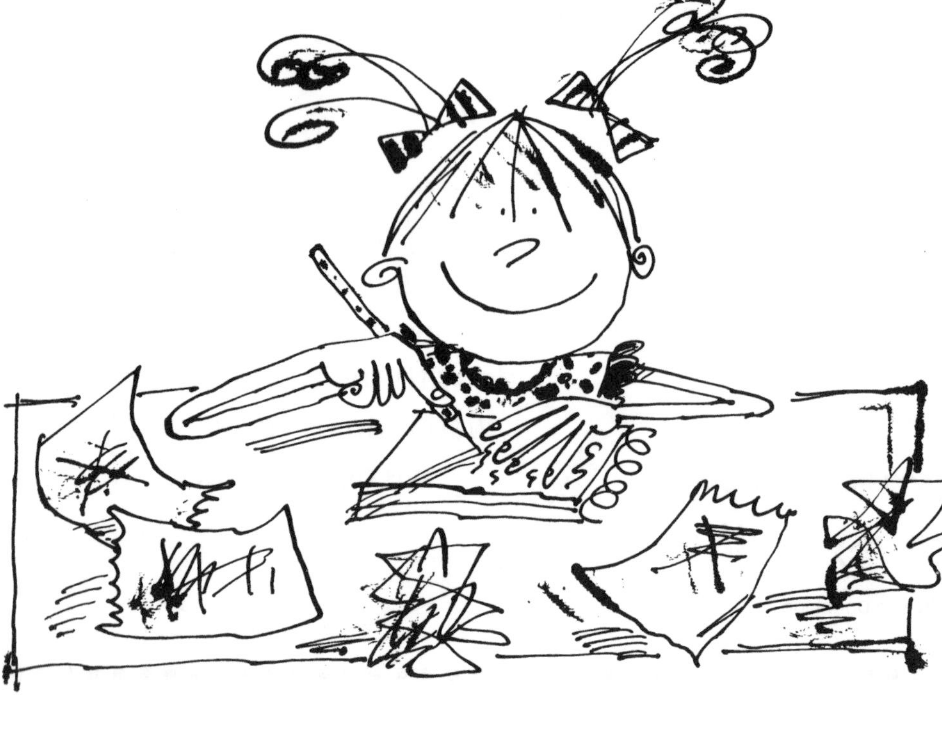

My mother
is a poem
I'll never be
able to write,
although
everything I
write is a poem
to my mother.

Sharon Doubiago

It's
not only children
who grow. Parents do
too. As much as we watch
to see what our children
do with their lives, they are
watching us to see what
we do with ours.

Joyce Maynard

Most of all the other beautiful
things in life come by twos and
threes, by dozens and hundreds.
Plenty of roses, stars, sunsets,
rainbows, brothers and sisters,
aunts and cousins, but only one
mother in the whole world.

Kate Douglas Wiggin

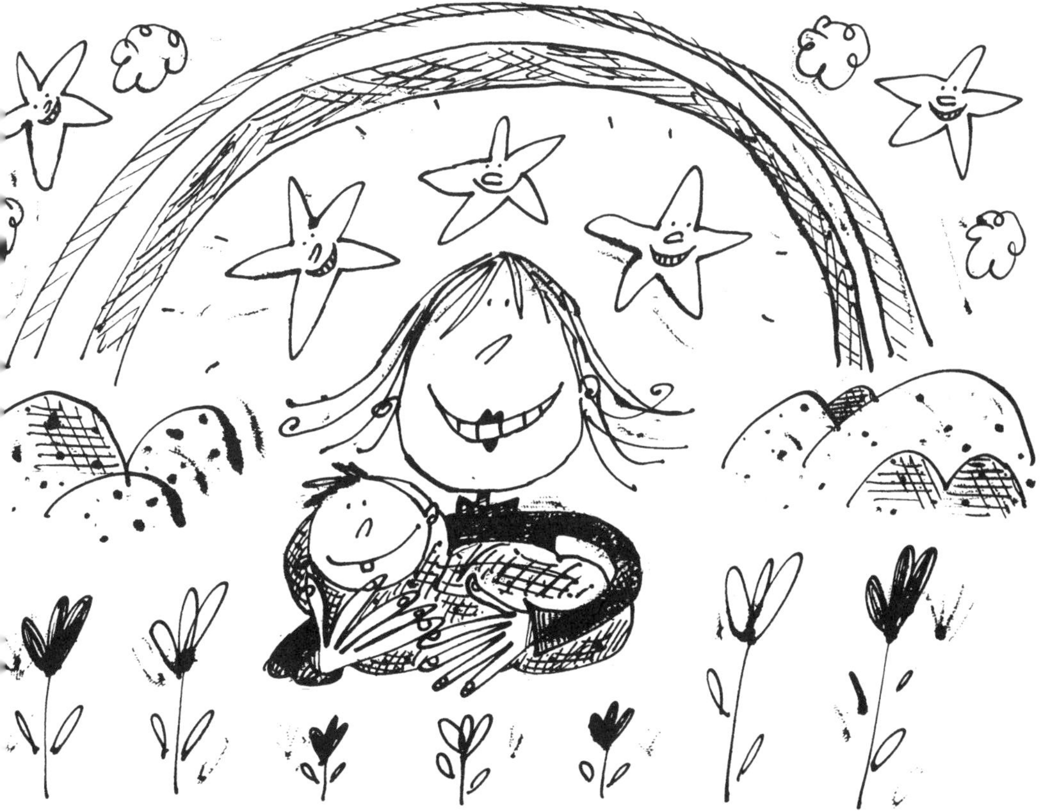